The Brown Teacher's Guide to Education

AN INTERACTIVE GUIDE FOR NEW AND
STRUGGLING TEACHERS

L. CHATMAN

WITH CONTRIBUTIONS BY:

A. NIKKI, BALDWIN, D., BARNES, M., BUTLER, T.,
DANIELS, B., HARRIS, A.,HARRIS, F., MALDONADO,
D., MORENO, B., V.N., V.Y.

The Brown Teacher's Guide to Education

Published by: Sunlitheart Publishing Services

Website: Sunlitheart.com

Instagram: Sunlitheart Publishing

Facebook: Sunlitheart Publishing Services

Edited by: Make Your Mark Publishing

Website: https://www.makeyourmarkps.com

Journal Pages Designed By: Brianna Moreno

Social Media Contact: @firstlatinxeducator

Email:bmore007@ucr.Edu

Book Designed by: Opeyemi Ikuborije

Email: ikuborijeoopeyemi@gmail.com

Book Contributors By Last Name

*Please be aware that some names have been changed at the request of the contributor in order to maintain their privacy. Some contributors wanted to be identified by their initials only.

1. A. Nikki,
2. Baldwin, D.,
3. Barnes, M.,
4. Butler, T.,
5. Daniels, B.,
6. Harris, A.,
7. Harris, F.,
8. Maldonado, D.,
9. Moreno, B.,
10. V.N.,
11. V.Y.

Thank you to each and every contributor for your candid contribution.

The Welcome Letter

Congratulations! Take a deep breath and relax. The long nights, student loans, advisement appointments, exam fees, and syllabi have all led up to this very moment. You are now ready to enter your role as an educator. I have stood in your shoes and know the burning excitement and anticipation that you feel. My first piece of advice is for you to enjoy every single moment of your journey as an educator. As you prepare to take the leap into your career and pursue your passion, there are many factors to consider. This anthology will provide you with a fresh perspective in contrast to the books I have read throughout my education, which were filled with the infamous "teacher jargon."

This book is designed to read like a real conversation with experienced colleagues. It is comprised of interviews with talented educators who have taken the time to write candidly about their experiences. Educators were encouraged to share as much about their personal experience as they saw fit. This was done through a series of interview questions. Some teachers did not want to use their legal name. They wanted the freedom to speak their truth without judgement. I am certain you will find their advice useful as you embark on your journey.

You will have a tremendous impact on the lives of your students and their families. To have a great experience, you have to know your purpose and find a school that fits your philosophy on education. Your initial experiences in the profession will have a profound impact on your outlook. Be mindful of where you student teach and be even more selective about the first teaching position you accept. Speak up if you feel you are not being provided with the tools you need to succeed. The following section takes an in depth look at my experience in education. I share the lessons that I have learned over the last nine years and some advice to help you on your journey.

An Open Letter to the Struggling Educator

You may have dedicated the last few years of your life to this profession, only to be left feeling completely empty. I've stood in your shoes as well. It's important for you to take time to reflect on what moves you should make next. This book of experiences will give you some critical factors to consider when selecting a school.

It will feel empowering to look for school districts that align with your belief system and allow you to develop professionally and thrive. It can get better if you are proactive in your search for the perfect fit. The following interviews will give you some important factors to consider as you move forward. Be sure to utilize the journal prompts for reflection.

Lessons from Student Teaching

In hindsight, I did not have the best student teaching experience. I went to college in Carbondale, Illinois, a smaller town about five hours south of Chicago. There were not many forward-thinking conversations happening in that region, and as a result, I was at a disadvantage when applying for positions after college. Although I was well-prepared academically, there were other critical aspects of teaching I simply had never discussed in depth during my courses. We had one course that briefly discussed social justice topics, and as I spoke with other graduates from different regions, it became apparent to me that they were more equipped to deal with the social justice issues that impacted students across the country. To put it simply, there were many strategies, educational terms, and new interventions I was never taught. In addition to this, I worked in a school that did not reflect my values as an educator. It took me five years to find a district that fit my teaching style and gave me space to grow.

It is critical to research districts and assess their culture. Spend time reading their website, identifying the district mission, and talking to people who know the district firsthand. Be advised, everyone's experiences in a particular setting will be different; however, it is still valuable to have some perspective prior to signing your contract. It may take you some time to find a school that allows you to grow professionally. Be patient.

All That Glitters Isn't Gold

When I graduated from college, I was newly married and wanted to distance myself as much as possible from my hometown. I decided I wanted to teach in a small town in the mountains of North Carolina. The picturesque mountain views and moderate temperatures drew me right in. I was invited to a recruitment initiative aimed at hiring minority teachers. They paid for our hotel, purchased our food, and gave us an extensive tour of what the city had to offer. It felt like the perfect place to work, and it also seemed to have a diverse population. The tour guide was an African American man with a Doctorate, who worked with at-risk students. The human resource personnel also seemed diverse. Despite the show they put on, there were little to no black professionals in this area and I had no idea what I was going to be up against. During those two years, I learned the true meaning of a "right-to-work state."

"Right-to-work" states do not have unions. You are not under contract and can be released at any time without reason. This was in 2012, so the laws may have evolved since then, but without contracts, school districts have more authority over their employees. The demand placed on educators is high across the board, but without unions, it can seem unbearable. The mandatory meetings, after-school events, lack of planning time, reduced lunch breaks, and increased class sizes create even more of a strain. I remember my friend and fellow educator warning me about how different life would be in the South. Still, I was not prepared for the culture shock.

During my first year of teaching, I was sitting in a meeting, and my principal turned to me and asked how we could get black parents to be more involved. I remember feeling so uncomfortable with being asked to be a spokesperson for my race in front of the entire staff. She then suggested we serve them "chicken and biscuits." Completely aghast, I looked around the room, and I wanted so badly to walk out. Much to my surprise, many of the teachers nodded their heads in agreement. Needless to say, at the next school function, they served chicken and biscuits. These were the types of comments that were acceptable to say to black professionals. As I got to know her, I realized she was incredibly unaware of how offensive that comment really was. Unfortunately, that was not the last time I encountered that type of situation.

The same year, during a team meeting, a teacher referred to me as the "other kind of black, not the ghetto black." Once again, I sat in disbelief, wondering why someone would make a statement like that in a professional setting. I felt a surge of heat go through me. I was so offended, but I knew reacting in the wrong way would only perpetuate her stereotypes. This is often the pressure we face as black professionals. I did not have the bandwidth to calmly articulate how deeply offensive that was. I went home, vented, cried, and regretted my decision to move to the South.

If you encounter these types of comments, make it a teachable moment. Give your coworkers a lesson on diversity, equity, and inclusion. It is not solely your job to do this; they should be doing the work as a district to systematically address these problems. The Caucasian people who lived in those mountains were vastly different from the people I grew up around in the suburbs of Chicago. I should have explained to them that using terms like "ghetto black" is offensive. You may find it ridiculous that you have to have these conversations;

however, keep in mind that some people are coming from a very limited background. Teach them that you—yes, you, a professional fluent in the language of opportunity—don't represent your entire race. This is a prime example of why conversations about implicit bias and stereotypes are critical in our professional development sessions. Many of the districts who advertise "diversity and inclusion" are simply hiring black and brown faces to post their photos on their websites.

When you are in an interview, ask them how they train their staff on these topics and what tools they use to create culturally responsive learning environments. I have learned that many of these districts are not actually doing the work of educating their staff on what these terms truly mean. They are simply creating some poorly constructed professional development sessions with buzzwords in the title. These sessions are usually done once a year and have no continuing professional development plan attached.

For instance, I attended a session centered on diversity two years ago. We were given some articles to read at my table, then were told to discuss the articles with our group. Naturally, the teachers were disengaged. I was so disappointed. Many of my colleagues expressed deep disappointment across the district. It was comforting to me that even though they weren't people of color, they wanted to see these topics discussed. Some districts are genuinely doing the work, while others are simply doing the bare minimum to meet a state requirement. You will quickly learn the difference between the two. My best friend, who is a principal, always tells me we have to believe people can change. That approach will guide the work we do and our level of dedication to it.

The Worst Year Was the Best Year

One year after my daughter was born, I was desperate for a job. I was hired the last week of July, and I had no time to really think about what school culture would fit my needs as an educator. It was my third year teaching, and I had accepted a fifth grade position an hour from where I grew up. The demographics of my new district also contributed to the stressful environment. The community was predominantly white, middle-class families. There were few people of color, and the parent population was very high-needs. A high-needs parent population can stress you out even more than an environment with little to no parental involvement. The level of involvement created a very high-stress work culture. Always consider the community when contemplating applying to a district.

There I was, trying to balance motherhood, marriage, and working in a new school and in a new state. I was assigned a mentor, and I thought this would serve as a positive force in my professional development. However, it catapulted me into the absolute worst year I had so far as an educator. The mentor I confided in was, in fact, a family friend of the principal. I didn't know this for quite some time, but she had known her since she was a child! As you can imagine, this put me in a rather precarious situation. I noticed my principal was frequently coming into my room and seemed very suspicious of everything I did. I thought the conversations about the areas where I was struggling were confidential, but in fact, they were being shared with my principal. When you're new to a building, you must learn the culture. Figure out who you can trust, and give it some time before you start candidly sharing opinions or information. I don't recall ever saying anything negative about the principal, but I was definitely struggling in some areas professionally and personally.

My team relationships were strained the entire year. They held meetings without my knowledge, then accused me of not being a team player. Oftentimes, I wasn't even aware of teamwide initiatives taking place. Eventually, I had to file a formal complaint with the union, which made the environment even more hostile. However, the union took my side and spoke on my behalf. I had a medical emergency that landed me on an extended leave for several weeks, and during my leave, my principal and team had meetings about me. They called me on speakerphone without telling me there were multiple people listening. During my leave, my principal even showed up at my house, with books, and asked me to lesson plan. I was in a robe and still had my hospital band on. My family was completely shocked by the lack of ethics and unprofessional behavior. I consulted with other teachers outside of my district and soon realized I was being targeted. I didn't know how to connect with the staff or my administration. It was the wrong "fit" in every sense of the word. Ultimately, I had to accept responsibility that I didn't do any research about the school. I went in completely blind. I was a new mother in a new state, and I was focused solely on income.

Due to this experience, I stopped trying to form relationships. I felt completely defeated. I had frequent anxiety and panic attacks, and all I could do was count the days until the end of the school year. I started applying for jobs but was too afraid to tell my principal, so when she got the call, it was an awkward conversation. I had no clue how to even approach the topic of leaving. I felt trapped, but in reality, I had so many options. I decided to go into an English Language Learner (ELL) resource position in a different district. Truthfully, I nearly quit teaching after that experience.

The best thing about this experience was that I made a close friend whose story you will read in this book. No matter how bad a school may be, there is always a lesson to be learned. I learned how to navigate a difficult school culture and have tough professional conversations.

Peace of Mind Is the Ultimate "Bag"

Secure your peace of mind before securing "the bag." Yes, you read that correctly. "Securing the bag" refers to making decisions for financial gain. I was so focused on finding a job at some points in my career that I overlooked some rather obvious red flags. Make sure you ask the right questions during your interview process. Remember, you don't just want to be chosen; you also need to make an informed decision. Talk to other people in the community about the school and ask your interview team honest questions. It can feel intimidating to ask questions during your interview, but it is necessary to make an informed decision.

When I left that challenging third year of teaching, I took a job in one of the most affluent districts in my state. When I signed that contract, I was on cloud nine. While I had better team relationships, I was still unhappy. I resigned in December before I even had another job lined up. I accepted that job based on the prime location and the higher salary. I still had not learned the value of finding a school culture that would allow me to thrive. The environment was stressful, and I felt immediate relief when I resigned. At one post-conference, my principal said I had done well but that I "just didn't have it." Initially, I was crushed. I took an impromptu trip to Miami to destress and build up enough courage to finish the year. I realize now she was absolutely right. I didn't have the capacity to work for an institution I did not believe in. The expectations were very rigid and there was little to no room for autonomy. I was teaching from an inauthentic place, and it was agonizing. I made many mistakes during those initial years, and I hope to help you avoid some of those same pitfalls.

Beware of the Color-Blind Approach

Rather than provide quality equity training, some districts take the color-blind approach. This is the idea that we should not consider the ethnicity or culture of those around us. It implies that we should stick to a one-size-fits-all method when interacting with different ethnicities. The goal of this mindset is to eliminate any prejudice or cultural bias in our interactions with staff and students. While this thought process may seem noble and beneficial on the surface, it can actually lead to many issues in a school setting.

Every person feels some form of cultural bias. As educators, it is critical we confront our own cultural biases. Putting on our blinders and feeling we are the "same" is not the way to create a more inclusive school culture. Many times, having discussions about culture or race makes people very uncomfortable. Subsequently, districts may not want to do the work. These are the districts you want to avoid. It is only by working through these feelings of discomfort that we can begin to peel back the layers of our bias and start to change the dynamics that exist within our schools.

One of the most profound moments of my education was during my first semester of graduate school. On the screen, my professor displayed slides of students of various ethnicities. We had to quietly write down our thoughts about each student. Reading my own reactions and hearing the thoughts of the fellow teachers around me was eye-opening. For the remainder of the class, we participated in deep self-reflection and had uncomfortable conversations about how we perceived different cultures. We talked about how the media, the entertainment industry, and our own experiences have shaped our views. I left feeling a deeper level of self-awareness, and I was able to consciously begin to change my mindset and interactions with certain ethnicities. Prior to that activity, I would have very easily described myself as "color-blind" and went on to discuss how a person's color does not impact my view of who they are. This is simply not true. We all have experiences, and those experiences shape our worldview. We have to make a conscientious effort to confront and change our bias.

Our ethnicities are an important part of who we are because they impact our customs and experiences. My afro-textured hair, full lips, and melanin-rich skin are some of the characteristics that make me who I am. I have no desire for my features or personality traits to be ignored. The color of my skin *does* impact my experience as a woman and as an educator.

As you step into the role of educator, inspire your students to learn about and embrace one another's heritage. More importantly, confront your own bias and find a district that values diversity, equity, and inclusion work.

The Right "Fit"

In 2016, I finally had enough perspective and self-awareness to think about what I wanted in a school district. I realized I had to be extremely selective about what I wanted if my career was going to change.

I had accepted a position twelve miles from my residence, but I knew the district was not a good fit. I was initially hired by human resources at a job fair, and I was going to be placed in a school that had an opening. This was an immediate red flag. This hiring system did not allow me the opportunity to interview with my team or the building principal. It is important to meet the team and the principal before accepting a position. At that point in my career, I had to ask some tough questions before accepting a position. When I toured the school, it was immediately evident that it was not the right fit. I continued to interview in hopes of securing something better before the fall. August came quickly. I finally received a phone call to interview at a school that was sixty miles from my home. The distance made it a more difficult choice, but it was a much better fit. During the interview, the administration asked about my professional goals and how their program could contribute to my growth. It was the first time I felt that my leadership would invest in me personally and professionally. It was the best decision I made. I was finally in an environment where I was comfortable taking risks because I was supported.

For two years, I worked on my Spanish language proficiency. I passed the state exam to become a certified Spanish Bilingual teacher.

My administration supported me wholeheartedly throughout this endeavor. I was given many opportunities to practice my Spanish, and it gave me so much confidence. I applied for a new role as the Spanish reading interventionist. I did not feel qualified, but I was encouraged to seize this opportunity for growth.

My leadership team was able to see potential in me that I was unable to see in myself. Effective leadership will create a supportive environment that encourages its employees to take risks that lead to a stronger school culture, which ultimately benefits the students. Working for that administrative team gave me the confidence that I needed to reach out for more experiences and develop my Spanish language skills. In short, these effective leaders changed my life, and I so thankful for their insight. Thank you Jill Zapata and Mayra Johnson for pushing me beyond what I believed I was capable of.

Critical Advice To Remember

1. Every school will have a different set of norms. While it is good to be yourself, you will need to make an effort to adjust to the culture, no matter where you are.

2. Culture is *not* skin-deep. I repeat, culture is *not* skin-deep. This means working in an all-black-and-brown school district is not the solution to your problems. Sharing the same skin color with someone does not mean you will automatically bond or feel accepted.

3. Don't blame the parents for everything. Maximize the time you have with your students and take accountability for your role in their success.

4. Know your professional rights and ask questions. Read your contract!

5. Listen to other teachers who have experience navigating similar spaces. Learn from them.

6. Stay student-focused. They are the reason we chose to teach and the reason we show up every day. Make sure your conversations and goals are all for the benefit of the students.

REFLECTION

Lebia Chatman

WHICH PARTS OF HER
INTRODUCTION
WERE EYE-OPENING TO YOU?

The following interview was submitted by Y.V., a speech and language pathologist with eight years of experience in the Chicagoland area.

Why did you decide to become an educator?

Not many people know this about me, but I didn't learn how to read until the third grade. Let me repeat myself: *third* grade. This is the grade when students are expected to read short novels and are taught how to read from the text for information. My literacy skills were significantly behind that of my peers; however, my math skills were above that of my peers (except when it came to word problems). My lack of literacy skills affected my scores on school-wide assessments. Most importantly, it affected my overall self-esteem. I was practically reading at a kindergarten level. My parents tried their best to teach me how to read, but they mostly expected the school to teach me literacy skills. At home, I would cry every time they told me to "go and practice your reading."

I was in grade school around 1990 in a predominantly white, English-speaking school with few bilingual or brown Spanish-English-speaking students. Most teachers wrote me off as "confused from being bilingual," "mentally delayed," or "lazy." There was *one* teacher who took the time to build me up and actually taught me from ground zero, i.e., letter sounds, syllables, etc. She made a large impression on me and changed my world! In a matter of months, I went from reading English at a kindergarten level to a third grade level. She was the light at the end of my tunnel.

I have always wanted to be the light or advocate for someone else out there struggling. I sort of fell into the education realm but had always had the "teacher" gene and potential inside of me.

When you decided to become a teacher, were you aware of the statistics of minority vs. non-minority teachers?

I grew up in a household where both of my parents and a grandparent worked within the realm of education and were highly aware of the lack of minority teachers in rural suburban Illinois. They emigrated from the sunny beaches of Puerto Rico and landed splat in the middle of a cornfield in the Midwest (no, really, we lived next to a cornfield). Talk about a culture shock! In retrospect, I was actually lucky my parents and their friends introduced me to the culture of highly educated black and brown teachers, professors, administrators, lawyers, accountants, etc. who struggled with discrimination and very real forms of racism. Before social media, iPhones, and the internet at your fingertips, my parents and their coworkers/friends would take turns eating at each other's homes, talking about their homelands, listening to music, discussing politics, and confiding in one another. They basically were their own social networks, and through each other, they coped with being a minority in their workplace, neighborhood, or overall surroundings. I'm grateful the world has become a bit more tolerant of diversity since those days; however, it was these early childhood experiences that heightened my senses to the lack of minorities or representation in academic institutions.

By the time I got to college, I felt as if all eyes were on me. I was one of a few minority students going into the field of secondary health education. Many topics that we talked about in class were public health concerns that affected, and continue to affect, predominantly black and brown communities. My college of education professors praised my "unique" point of view or "creative and insightful" ideas. I often wondered if they saw me as a colorful peacock in a cage full of pigeons— at least that's the way I decided to see things. I always knew I was different. I couldn't help but think I should be studying other professions given the lack of diversity in my education classes, but I later realized the lack of Latina female students was actually seen across many educational programs at the university level.

When I got out into the "real" world and began working, it was apparent to me that I was a rarity. Being a minority with a degree started to work in my favor, as administrators were so eager to have a minority teacher in their building. I will never forget when I first heard the term "token" (single representative of a minority group) by a white coworker who reminded me of my place in the paradigm of the building. I was the token minority teacher of the building. I had always had high expectations of myself and put in hard work while working with students, teams, and parents. This term "token" stuck with me for years to come. This is when I began to educate myself on the statistics, and the numbers were hard to see. When I went back to school for my Master's in Speech and Language Pathology, I saw that the percentage of minorities was even lower than that of teachers. I learned somewhere around 3.5% of speech therapists were minorities in 2009, and in 2019, it had grown to 8%, thanks to growing minority retention efforts at the national level. I am hopeful these numbers will continue to climb!

Was it your mission to serve a specific demographic (children in poverty, rural/urban environments, ELLs, special education, etc.)?

After my life experiences and my desire to be an advocate, I made it my mission to work with minority students and later found my calling as a bilingual (Spanish-English) speech and language pathologist for students learning English as a second language (ESL). My first "real" job was in a predominantly bilingual and minority school district forty minutes west of Chicago. Well, actually, my first teaching job was for the Chicago Public School system, and it lasted one month. I was let go, along with other teachers and staff, after the school was shut down due to budget cuts. During the time I worked in the Chicagoland suburbs, I could count on one hand how many teachers were minorities in a school that serviced predominantly black and Latino students. I saw how those students struggled with years' worth of language delays or deficits (reduced vocabulary, receptive language skills, and expressive oral or written skills) and felt motivated to do more. It inspired me to make a radical decision to resign from my full-time teaching job at the end of the school year and go back to university for my master's in speech and language pathology.

In my mind, language, cognition, and communication abilities were at the core. After I graduated with my master's, I worked predominantly for a minority and bilingual school district in the suburbs of Chicago. I loved working with the students but became tired of the lack of professional support, resources, and opportunities for growth within the organization. I tried working in an affluent community clinic after feeling like I was just a small change in a big world, but I missed the big smiles of my less fortunate students. I also missed the grateful spirits of parents who appreciated my help. I made a conscious decision to return to that original school district under different parameters to services those same type of minority, ESL, and impoverished students.

What has been the most rewarding part of your experience as a minority teacher?

The most rewarding part of being a minority in the school setting is servicing the students and families who need it most. Also, I love being an advocate for those families behind closed conference doors and seeing the progress my students make. If I had to pick a moment, I would say it was during my first year of teaching. At the time, I was not much older than my students and was amazed at their ability to face their adversities and move forward. My health education class and topics gave me special previews into their homes, lives, and experiences. I learned that most of my students had firsthand experiences with drugs, death, sex, and many more things I had yet to experience or ever see. The students had to pass my class to graduate from high school.

In one class, I had a smart and intelligent sixteen-year-old student. After a lesson on abstinence-only sex education (I personally do not recommend this for teenagers, but there were district regulations in place for this topic). She confided in me, sharing that she was a few months pregnant and was terrified about the rest of her life. I saw her great potential and vowed to help her finish my class (and any other classes she needed help with). I sent her home with the assignments every week and would talk on the phone with her to check up on any concerns. At the end of the semester, she passed the department final exam and passed my class! I'm happy to say she finished high school, with a baby and all.

What has been the most challenging part of your experience as a minority in education?

I struggle from time to time with what I have heard as "imposter syndrome." I have read that this actually affects more women than men and is highest among successful people who do not feel they are worthy of their success. There are times when that illiterate nine-year-old girl comes to light, and I have to suppress those feelings. I have to remind myself to stay authentic and be proud of how much I have accomplished. I have learned to make my own kind of beautiful in the world, and I now have my own business consulting with school districts and providing specialized bilingual speech and language services. To be honest, I have had both successes and failures within the workplace that attribute to those feelings of "Am I doing enough?" or "Am I enough?" At times, this can be a real struggle, depending on my work site or coworkers.

Also, as a minority educator, I feel what is referred to as the "brown tax," which can only be described as this ever-looming feeling that I have to work twice as hard, be twice as good, and be more on top of things than my white counterparts. I am often complimented on "how well" I write or my "nice" speaking skills, as if it is a surprise to everyone. This can be demoralizing at times. What no one will tell you about are the ever-present institutional racism, microaggressions, and stereotype biases that continue to affect the school workplace due to the lack of diversity at the administration level.

How do you determine if the culture of a building is a good fit for you?

You can tell if the culture of the building is a good fit for you by listening to your gut, that little feeling in your throat or stomach that goes off like an alarm when you sit down in an interview with teachers and staff members. Take note of how the administrators speak to you and other teachers; note their body language and non-verbal cues. Take a look around the halls. What do you see? Go on their website. Is it a diverse workplace that actually celebrates diversity, or is it going to only be you and the night cleaning crew who look the same? I don't always get to pick my buildings or school sites, but I am very cautious in my interactions with staff if I notice a few red flags.

First, I can't be the only brown Latina/o person in the building. I have tried this in the past, and it has not worked for me. If the staff is not diverse or if there is not an appreciation for diverse cultures, races, religions, etc., my dear reader, you alone are not going to change it, and it's going to be a *long* year. Next, will you have a mentor? If your building is not diverse, is there an association or group for minorities in your district where you can meet with others? I'm grateful and lucky to say that at one of the educational placements I stayed at the longest, they have a Bilingual Speech and Language Pathology department where they meet regularly and provide each other with support. At the end of the day, you will need support in the setting, wherever you see yourself on the continuum of brown/black. I wish you all the best, and know that in the words of Oprah, "When you know better, you do better."

List three rules or pieces of advice you would give to a minority teacher entering the education field or struggling to find their way in the field.

1. Get used to the fact that by you simply standing there, you are going to ruffle some feathers. It's OK! Embrace it and learn to accept it. Be authentically yourself because if you are going to fail, at least you did it while being yourself.

2. Find joy in the little things each day. I keep little memos and pictures from students and keep in contact with supportive coworkers.

3. Keep a detailed journal of your experiences. One day, you will want to look back and see how much growth and progress you have made. Also, this will serve as a point of reference if you ever have to stand up for yourself or others when dealing with racial inequality or injustice.

REFLECTION

y. V.

WHICH PART
OF HER STORY IMPACTED
YOU THE MOST?

WHICH PIECE OF
ADVICE DO YOU THINK
WILL HELP YOU THE MOST
DURING YOUR CAREER?

The following interview was conducted with Melodee Barnes. Melodee has twenty four years of experience in Early Childhood Education. She is an innovator and tech lover! She has immersed herself in the ever changing world of education and uses technology to push boundaries and open doors for marginalized families. Contact information: famlynuggets.com

Why did you decide to become an educator?

I became an educator to have weekends off after working in retail and the restaurant industry. I honestly didn't have a goal past that. I had only seen my siblings work retail and both parents work in a profession that required weekend work. I was fascinated by having Saturdays and Sundays as days of rest. I imagined all the things I could do with a weekend that I had never seen my family do before me. I had no idea I would actually fall in love with teaching, the children, and their families. I had so much fun going to work every day because I was surrounded by music, dancing, storytelling, laughing, and so much learning! I was hooked, and I was not going back!

When you decided to become a teacher, were you aware of the statistics of minority vs. non-minority teachers?

Absolutely not! My mentor teacher was black, and she was, and is, amazing! My school director was black, most of the teachers were black, and the kindergarten teacher was one of the best I had ever seen. I was happy to work with such a talented group of women. If anything, I felt like I was a nuisance because I was so young at the age of eighteen. However, they embraced and corrected me when needed, and to this day, many of us are friends.

Was it your mission to serve a specific demographic (children in poverty, rural/urban environments, ELLs, special education, etc.)?

I wanted to teach where I lived. Most students were black, like myself. I was looking forward to that. I still do.

What has been the most rewarding part of your experience as a minority teacher?

Having the support of other families who are accepting of my talent and work ethic.

What has been the most challenging part of your experience as a minority in education?

Knowing that other black teachers did not accept me and often mistreated me in places of employment.

How do you determine if the culture of a building is a good fit for you?

During the interview, I ask lots of questions, and after meeting with people and learning more about them, I decide how I want to have relationships move forward. The building is determined to be a good fit based on the relationships, the support of the administration, and the ability to have autonomy and growth when teaching the curriculum.

List three rules or pieces of advice you would give to a minority teacher entering the education field or struggling to find their way in the field.

1. Be yourself. Do not change who you are to try and fit in.

2. Do not discount what you know. You come with a wealth of knowledge, and you should never doubt what you bring to the table.

3. Leave if you're not happy.

Melodee Barnes

WHICH PART
OF HER STORY IMPACTED
YOU THE MOST?

WHICH PIECE OF
ADVICE DO YOU THINK
WILL HELP YOU THE MOST
DURING YOUR CAREER?

The following interview was conducted with Faith Harris. Faith has ten years of experience in education. She holds a Master's degree in Literacy and in Educational Leadership.

Why did you decide to become an educator?

I always enjoyed working with kids. It was always a huge passion of mine. As teachers, we have the ability to shape young minds and be a positive influence on their lives. I struggled as an elementary school student, but my teachers did not give up on me. They gave me extra help to ensure I caught up to my classmates.

In high school, I took a preschool lab class. Preschooler age kids came in for two hours a day, and I worked with the same preschooler each day for one class period. This was my first experience working with small children. It was very eye-opening for me, and I learned a lot. The next year, I became the independent studies coordinator, and I helped the first-year preschool lab students get all of their work done. That experience made me realize I knew what I was doing.

During my senior year of high school, I did a year-long internship. I left school early, went to an elementary school, and for the first half of it, worked in a third/fourth grade, multiage classroom. The teacher was really mean to me and sat me in the corner to grade work. She would leave piles of copies for me to make for the whole grade level. I only taught the few lessons that were required for my internship. I spent the second half of the internship in a kindergarten classroom. The teacher was much nicer and allowed me to teach and observe more lessons. This is when I knew for sure that early childhood was for me. I've never regretted this decision.

I also had a wonderful Spanish teacher in high school. He made learning so fun and enjoyable that you often forgot you were actually learning. He made me want to come to class each day.

When you decided to become a teacher, were you aware of the statistics of minority vs. non-minority teachers?

I was aware because I grew up in a town where there were almost no teachers of color. It was very rare to see.

Was it your mission to serve a specific demographic (children in poverty, rural/urban environments, ELLs, special education, etc.)?

I received the Golden Apple Scholars award during my senior year of high school. They helped pay for college and provided me with internships and seminars each summer during college. I learned so much from being a part of that program, and it was invaluable. Part of the requirement for being in the program was to teach for five years in a school of need. All of Chicago qualified for this, so that's why my teaching career began there. As a black woman who grew up in a white suburb all my life, it was a whole new world teaching babies who looked like me. The biggest adjustment was the level of parent support (really, the lack thereof) and the lack of resources the school had. After being mistreated for three years in charter schools, I could no longer take it. I decided to move back to the suburbs once I became pregnant with my son.

What has been the most rewarding part of your experience as a minority teacher?

Having black students look up to me because they see someone who looks like them succeeding and caring about them.

What has been the most challenging part of your experience as a minority in education?

Since there are not many black teachers at my school, I became the token black teacher. On the second day of my first year of teaching, the principal transferred a student into my classroom because the grandparent felt like her grandchild's teacher was racist. They chose me and wanted their child to be in my class. It was only the second day of school, and no one knew me. It was very clear to me that it was solely because I was black.

One time, a black parent cornered me at the mall and told me how much she wanted her son in my class because I was black. She went on for thirty minutes about how he needed to have a black teacher and blah, blah, blah. I immediately called the principal and told her that the child should not end up in my class just because I'm black.

One year, a black boy was having a hard time in class. His teacher was on maternity leave, and he was not bonding with the substitute. They felt he needed a connection with a black person. When they presented it to me, they made it seem like he just needed to take a break for fifteen minutes after recess before coming back to class. I later learned it was a racial thing. He was great in my classroom, and we formed a strong connection. It helped big picture, but it's still an issue that's constantly happening.

How do you determine if the culture of a building is a good fit for you?

When I first begin at a school, I tend to listen more than I speak. If you observe for long enough, you will see the true culture of a school. People can only put up a façade for so long. After I spend some time observing, I let people know that "I'm not the one!" I do not let people run all over me, even if that's how things are done. That changed a lot of things for me after my first year at my current school. I also tend to stay to myself and stay out of the drama. I stay in my classroom and get my work done. I keep my nose down and work.

List three rules or pieces of advice you would give to a minority teacher entering the education field or struggling to find their way in the field.

1. Find a mentor or someone you feel you can trust at your school.

2. Be a positive role model for your students of color.

3. Don't let your race/culture define who you are as a teacher. Be a great teacher because you've prepared for this and are ready, not because of the color of your skin. Race and culture, of course, play a part, but don't let people put you into a "box."

REFLECTION

Faith Harris

WHAT PART
OF HER
INTERVIEW
IMPACTED
YOU THE
MOST?

WHAT PIECE OF
ADVICE
DO YOU THINK
WILL HELP
YOU THE MOST
DURING YOUR
CAREER?

The following interview was conducted with Taryn R. Butler, Ed.S. She has taught grades six through twelve and is Florida Professional Certified in the following subject areas: English 5–9, English 6–12, Reading, Exceptional Student Education K–12, ESOL, Health K–12, and Family, Home & Consumer Science 6–12. Years of Experience: Sixteen years.

Why did you decide to become an educator?

The decision to become an educator was none of my own. I was kind of chosen for this line of work by the Creator above. How I landed in the profession was due to my parents, who were educators themselves. Upon my decision to attend college, I had to choose a major field of interest. It was my choice to major in the health services administration area, but my parents' suggestion was to choose education. Against their better judgement, I majored in health administration and chose a double minor in health sciences and education. I only chose the education minor to appease them. In my opinion, there were too many educators in the family, and I could hear myself saying, "I don't want to be a teacher."

Once I finished college and the coursework for my major (health services administration), I wasn't able to obtain a job in my intended area of study. So, my mother, who was the optimistic one, came home from work one afternoon with a packet of papers. She placed them on the table, told me to sit down, and proceeded to say, "The Lord said to fill out this application." I looked at the packet and said OK. With no hesitation, I completed the application and took it down to the school district office. Normally, once a completed packet is submitted, it takes up to a month to be cleared and approved. To my astonishment, my application was cleared and approved within two weeks flat. I was amazed and said, "Well, this is what the Lord wanted."

I started off teaching health in an alternative education setting for grades six through twelve, then worked my way into a comprehensive middle school, teaching seventh grade health, then advanced to another subject area (English) where I taught students who were learning disabled. I taught at the middle school level for eight years and taught all grades (six through eight). Over the summer, I taught English in the high school alternative education setting, grades nine through twelve. During those years of working in the classroom, I experienced a little burnout from pursuing my master's degree while working in those locations, so I decided to obtain positions outside the classroom, such as a curriculum specialist, curriculum facilitator, and now, an educational data district administrator. Between those positions, I also went back to graduate school to obtain my Educational Specialist degree and started the Doctoral program, all in the area of curriculum instruction and assessment, which now puts me working within the education system for sixteen years this coming December.

When you decided to become a teacher, were you aware of the statistics of minority vs. non-minority teachers?

Yes, upon coming into the education system, I did see the disproportionate number of black educators versus white educators. I also saw the disproportionate number of men versus women. While doing my master's in K–12 curriculum, I began to do the research on why the numbers of black versus white teachers were so out of sync. What I gathered from that research was that a number of motivational aspects contributed to the decline in numbers. The same goes for the gender disparities gaps.

Was it your mission to serve a specific demographic (children in poverty, rural/urban environments, ELLs, special education, etc.)?

To use the word "mission" is an understatement; I would say my "God-given purpose" is a better phrase. I believe God called me to teach, and I believe I can teach all kinds of children in any setting, but my area of effectiveness lies in working with children in Title 1 schools and schools in economically disadvantaged areas. I am particularly talented and gifted in those specific areas, and I believe a person's purpose in life is always connected to their giftedness.

What has been the most rewarding part of your experience as a minority teacher?

The most rewarding part of my career is seeing my students go on to become successful adults in life, watching them go from having a fear of learning to embracing it and developing skills to become lifelong learners.

What has been the most challenging part of your experience as a minority in education?

The most challenging aspect of my education career was breaking the glass ceiling for minority leadership advancements within my district. I am located in South Florida (Palm Beach County). We are the eleventh-largest district in the nation, and like most districts, we have had our fair share of negative experiences with promotions based on "who you know" and not "what you know." So I have faced challenges in obtaining a fair opportunity for career advancement based on my work experience and teaching credentials.

How do you determine if the culture of a building is a good fit for you?

For me, when trying to determine if a school's culture is an ideal setting for me, I consider the dynamics of the leadership/administration team. If I can see the dissension between the team members, I quickly know the school or district might not be the best fit for me. I was always taught to watch how the leadership/administration team interacted with the teachers and staff. Everyone must be on the same accord. As the biblical word states, "A house divided amongst itself shall not stand." The same goes for the leadership team at a school. A team divided among itself will ultimately fail. One must keep in mind that if the leadership, or the head, isn't operating right, then the staff, or the body, isn't going to function right, either. One can't function without the operation of the other, so I always base my decision on the functionality of the leadership team.

REFLECTION

Taryn R. Butler

WHICH PART
OF HER STORY IMPACTED
YOU THE MOST?

WHICH PIECE OF
ADVICE DO YOU THINK
WILL HELP YOU THE MOST
DURING YOUR CAREER?

The following open letter was completed by the "Espresso Educator." She has ten years of experience in public education. The format is creative and refreshing. The information is both honest and insightful.

Dear Espresso Educator,

I see you, girl, out here scratching and surviving! As an espresso educator myself, I want you to know you aren't alone out here in these academic streets.

Welcome. Welcome. Welcome.

I am so glad you are here! I have to ask, though: What team are you on? Are you here because you love children? Or are you here because you enjoy your summers off? Are you here just to become an administrator? What is your ultimate goal? Because in this profession, it will play a role in how you conduct yourself on a day-to-day basis.

Hopefully you aren't one of those sistas who sees yourself as better than the rest of us. I have met a few and let me tell you, while they have aspirations and goals like us, they take an alternate route that ends in self-destruction and the loss of their teaching identity. Figure out why you teach and let that guide you.

I want you to know you aren't alone, and I know, depending on where you are, you may feel like you are. You may be a random piece of pepper in a bowl full of salt—or not; you may be just one of the peppers in a well-seasoned school. Either way, there will be a day where you feel alone. You aren't.

There are a few things I want you to remember:

Develop yourself professionally

Be you! Don't subscribe to the things other teachers will frequently try to feed you. Know that you are smart. Other people's insecurities aren't your business. They will hate on you from time to time. Then, there will be days when all of your hard work and love are displayed during a grade-level data meeting, and they will play you to the left as if you just got lucky. Sometimes they'll say, "Oh, you must have got the high class." Don't kiss their butts. You aren't dumb. Continue to learn and grow. Don't get upset when they ask for your help, then fact-check you against their less-educated counterparts as if your words are figments of your imagination. You know your class. Take the data. Trust your data! Grade-level data is great, but *your* data helps you and your students. They are most important.

Don't burn out and lose yourself

Love yourself so you don't burn out. Hang in there. Teacher burnout is real! Self-love is mandatory. Stay calm in meetings when you share your awesomely amazing ideas and no one wants to try them out. Even though you have been to numerous trainings and have great success in your classroom, don't get upset when they shut your ideas down only for Becky to suggest the exact same thing five minutes later. They will welcome the challenge just because someone else said it, and the Trump-like teacher will probably treat you like Obama all year. Don't let it break you. Your students' growth will speak for itself.

Value your time

Don't feel like you have to be at school every waking moment. Value your time. Enjoy your summer, fall, winter, and spring breaks. You earned every. single. one. Your time is valuable. People will try to make you feel like you have to constantly be at school because you are new. You don't. Don't be no punk. And when the bell rings and you are left behind because you want to make sure everything is just right for tomorrow, don't be upset because other teachers left exactly on time. The same excuses they use to leave on time are the ones they will try to use to guilt you into staying. Don't drink the Kool-Aid.

Pick your team wisely because errbody ain't ya friend.

Get a mentor; they don't have to be at your school. Make friends with a teacher who has your best interest at heart. Don't make friends with negative Nancies and Neds. Don't be procrastination Patty, either. Don't feel like you have to participate in the bullcrap. Oh, and don't hang out in the teacher's lounge. They will try to suck you into all the negativity. Don't do it. Don't sit around and talk negatively about the children. It will hurt your feelings to hear adults talk about children that way. It sucks in the lounge, except when there are store-bought snacks and free stuff. Go in there for mail, copies, free food, and free items. Otherwise, keep it movin'.

Take off the mask

Find a new school if you can't be yourself. They will clique up and turn on you. Don't be surprised when you find out that while you have dreamed of being a teacher your entire life and your love of children can only be compared to your love of Christmas. Joan and Eric became teachers because they wanted to work in the medical field but couldn't stand the sight of blood and being off for the summer was a major perk. They won't love the children like you do. They won't take the time you take. Don't be upset when they confuse you for other espresso educators, even though you all are different heights with different hair colors, styles, and even different shades of mocha goodness. How someone can confuse you for someone else when they literally see you every single day is beyond me, but it happens … all the time.

Love the whole child

Put your children first. Don't try to be their friend. Don't try to be the cool teacher. Allow the students to know the real you. Love the children, and don't give up on them. There will be good days, and there will be bad days. There will also be great days when your hug seems to heal the world, when you become the coolest lady they know, when you hear the littles repeating your colloquialisms, when you get pointed out for being awesome, when the parents trust you enough to tell you all their business, and when the worst child for everyone else is the best child for you. When these things happen, you will know and understand that it matters. It all matters. Because *you* matter. You will know they need you when they get really excited and accidentally call you mom, TT, or grandma or, when on your worst day, they suddenly get it.

These things will help you stay focused during the school year. In your free time, reflect and plan. Things won't go perfect every day, but you will be successful. Thank you for loving the children. Thank you for your service. You are amazing, and the children will see the light and love in you. Believe in yourself. Have a great year!

Sincerely,

An Experienced Espresso Educator

Expresso Educator

WHICH PARTS
OF HER LETTER WERE
EYE-OPENING TO YOU?

The following interview was conducted with N.V. from the suburbs of Chicago. She is a Mexican American, first-generation college student and a bilingual special education teacher in her current district.

Why did you decide to become an educator?

I chose to become an educator because I love working with and helping kids. I remember getting my acceptance letters from universities and thinking, *What am I going to do?* Of course, my mom and dad wanted me to be a lawyer, doctor, or something extravagant. They told me that, with my grades and smarts, I could do anything. But I wanted to help kids in other ways. In my heart, I knew I wanted to be a teacher and help kids like my teachers helped me.

In elementary school, I had a teacher named Ms. Bussee. She helped me when I felt like a failure in school. I was reading three grade levels behind my classmates, and Ms. Bussee had me do extra reading, work with her individually, and complete a school program for reading. Six months later, I was at grade level! It showed me that progress does not happen overnight; it takes time, effort, and care. She is the reason I chose education as my career path. I chose special education because I knew I wanted to help other students reach their full potential and make progress toward their goals.

When you decided to become a teacher, were you aware of the statistics of minority vs. non-minority teachers?

I did not know about the statistics of minority vs. non-minority teachers when I chose to enter the field of education. I guess, in the back of mind, I already knew. I never had a teacher that looked like me, not even my Spanish teacher. Throughout my higher education, I was one of the few Latinas in the education program. I was one of two minorities in the special education program. I went into schools with a high Latino or black population and only saw non-minority teachers. I wanted students to be able to see themselves in their teachers and feel comfortable sharing their culture.

Was it your mission to serve a specific demographic (children in poverty, rural/urban environments, ELLs, special education, etc.)?

I had the wonderful opportunity to apply for the Golden Apple Scholarship and received it my senior year of high school. Their mission is to help students from low-income or low-performing schools improve school culture and bring new ideas. I wanted to help all students but especially students who were first-generation like me, who may not know the language. I wanted students to be proud of their culture (their food, language, clothes, and background). I wanted to help other teachers learn how to reach a student, even if they did not share their language, and help them see how bright and smart they are. Many times, bilingual students are labeled as special needs because of the language barrier. Many schools are not able to test them or provide accommodations in Spanish or their native language.

What has been the most rewarding part of your experience as a minority teacher?

When students get excited that you know their language and culture, they know they can share their experiences with you without judgement or fear of being different. I love seeing my students make progress in their academics, language, and social-emotional abilities.

What has been the most challenging part of your experience as a minority in education?

I have lived, went to school, and taught in places where the majority was always white; usually over seventy-five percent of the population was white. I remember people who did not know me or other Latino people would tell me I was acting "white." I found that we are sometimes our worst critics with this preconceived notion that you have to act or talk a certain way to be perceived as a true "Latina." I have been lucky to work with teachers who respect me for my knowledge and experiences rather than judge me. I am not naïve to the fact that, behind closed doors, people may not like my ideas, language, or culture. I have not yet had a professional problem with anyone in my buildings; however, socially, just like my students, I cannot always share everything because of a fear of my background being judged. Now, don't get me wrong, I have developed some wonderful relationships with my team and coworkers, and I occasionally share my problems/needs, but it's hard to feel comfortable enough to talk about certain things, like family outside of the U.S., the hardships of being Latina, and my family's milestones when the other person doesn't come from the same background or life as me.

How do you determine if the culture of a building is a good fit for you?

I think you need to know yourself, your teaching style, and your teaching philosophy so you can line up your beliefs with a school's beliefs. However, you still need to be open to other people's beliefs and styles because it may change your point of view. At the very least, your core values need to line up with your school's core values. You need to have a place where you feel you can grow as a person and an educator!

List three rules or pieces of advice you would give to a minority teacher entering the education field or struggling to find their way in the field.

1. Find a group of people you can share your struggles, thoughts, accomplishments, and growths with.

2. Don't surround yourself with negativity. It is so easy to join in on the complaining and frustration with no problem-solving (I think we're all guilty of that).

3. The right school will come along, and sometimes it takes a while to find it.

REFLECTION

n. v.

WHICH PART
OF HER STORY IMPACTED
YOU THE MOST?

WHICH PIECE OF
ADVICE DO YOU THINK
WILL HELP YOU THE MOST
DURING YOUR CAREER?

This interview was conducted with Brianna Moreno (@firstgenlatinxeducator). She has taught high school English (grades 9–12), ELD, and Creative Writing/Graphic Design. She has four years of experience.

Why did you decide to become an educator?

There are two important reasons why I decided to become an educator. The first reason being my desire to teach ever since I was five years old. Like many, I "played teacher" quite often as I sat family and friends around a table to learn. I grew up with passionate teachers who I admired greatly because of their patience and support. This admiration drove me to want to be just like them. My interests then began to align with those experiences and interactions. As I grew older, I also wanted to be an artist. I loved to draw, paint, take photos, and create artwork. I became exposed to so many careers, but I knew I wanted to teach at the primary level. This would allow me to combine my love for literature and the arts; it was the perfect career. This passion for teaching only got clearer when I joined AmeriCorps my first year as an undergraduate student. I witnessed the urgency in students receiving the resources and services they needed. Students' educational gaps were more apparent than ever. I saw myself as someone who could help make positive changes to the field that would ensure students receive the help they needed.

Secondly, I wanted to become an educator because I come from a family of immigrants. Both of my parents picked up the little belongings they had, left their families behind, and made it to the U.S. when they were just teenagers. My Ma left El Salvador, and my Pa left Mexico. My parents made it very clear that education would open up so many opportunities for me. They wanted me to succeed and see the benefits of being a U.S. citizen. My parents instilled in me the value of education as a driving force toward change, change for myself and change for my community. Although I attended school with classmates with similar backgrounds, I realized a very large percentage of them struggled with their academics, which greatly impacted their options for life post-high school. I knew that somewhere in their K–12 education something failed, and that failure was not them as students. The system in place failed the people I loved the most, people with big hearts and dreams, dreams that ended the same day the system, educators, and peers stopped believing in them. When someone stops believing in your ability to contribute to society, they're essentially gatekeeping supports and access to resources. I decided to become a teacher to think critically about youth-centered pedagogies, to ask important questions, to shift the current power dynamics, and ultimately create change through advocacy and policy for our community.

When you decided to become a teacher, were you aware of the statistics of minority vs. non-minority teachers?

I was not aware of the statistics, but it did not take much to see that the field of education is made up of mostly white people, specifically, white women. I majored in English, and even there, the literary texts we read were not as diverse as I had previously thought they were. There were some exceptions, but the classes that were diverse and challenged dominant narratives were the elective classes. Going through my graduate program for a master's degree in education and a single-subject teaching credential provided the actual data that only reinforced what I, and many others, already knew to be true. I attended a university that highlighted its vision for a more diverse and inclusive campus which required students to take classes aimed towards expanding our racial literacy. Macro- and micro-aggressions are deeply rooted in our current education system and our university made it their mission to have us gain that awareness. This was done in hopes of changing the current climate on campuses across Southern California. I would strongly advise for future educators to look into programs that specifically outline their Anti-Bias/Anti-Racist (ABAR) goals because it shows how intentional they are about the outcomes of their community and most importantly, are holding themselves accountable for the shortcomings they may display.

Was it your mission to serve a specific demographic (children in poverty, rural/urban environments, ELLs, special education, etc.)?

I always had a specific vision of the students I wanted to serve. My mission was to teach in the area I grew up in, the Inland Empire, so I was well aware of the demographics there. I knew I wanted to serve in a school that had students from all academic backgrounds as well. I was very motivated to work at a continuation school with students who are categorized as "at-risk youth." I grew up with a niece with special needs which ultimately prompted me to pursue a credential in teaching students with special needs. I was very passionate about helping students who required IEPs, were on a 504 plan, or needed any other accommodations. However, I ended up pursuing a credential to teach English at the secondary level. My ultimate goal was to apply what I learned in school to the same community I grew up in.

What has been the most rewarding part of your experience as a minority teacher?

I always found it conflicting to refer to educators like myself as a "minority" teacher. The more we study history, the more we begin to think about the erasure of BIPOC and how the oppression has led to the minoritization of the Global Majority. In this case, me being minoritized, I see the various obstacles in the workplace, but also, see the positives of having someone like myself, work alongside students (within the demographics of my current site). It has been rewarding to witness the importance of representation. For many of my students, I am their first "first-generation, Mexican and Salvadorian" teacher. I was taken aback by the outpour of love my students displayed and the feelings they would share with me about feeling seen, heard, and understood. This is something my students and I had in common! They too, made me feel seen, heard, and understood. We could quickly exchange some jokes in Spanish and make references to novelas, our tios and tias, and expand the academic world to include us-- Latinx students and teachers. My students and I have definitely turned to one another for support to discuss generational trauma, imposter syndrome, instances of discrimination or racism, the struggles of being undocumented or having undocumented familiy members, and the list goes on. Although my students and I share the difficulties of being minoritized, my classroom has been filled with joy and laughter for things that were never taught in school, but were experienced outside of the classroom, in our homes and community.

What has been the most challenging part of your experience as a minority in education?

One of the most challenging parts of being a minoritized teacher is coming into work and coming face-to-face with your past traumas. It is experiencing triggers throughout the day and not knowing exactly how to cope with them, mainly because your work day does not give you any downtime. It is closing your classroom door and having to sit there and cry because your students are suffering from the same experiences you went through as a child. It is thinking deep into your family's history and thinking critically about prejudice, racism, generational trauma, sexism, issues that arise from being a first-generation student, etc. Unfortunately, this profession has teachers working in isolation. Teacher interactions, let alone teacher collaboration, are so slim. You spend most of your time closed off in your room, completing a list of tasks (lesson planning and grading are at the bottom of this list, and not by choice). There are many unintended consequences you simply have to brush aside for the sake of taking care of your own mental health. You become an advocate for a long list of issues and it can become extremely overwhelming as it feels like you are the only one carrying all of this on your own. It definitely has been difficult building the strength to stand up for myself which has proven to be far more difficult than standing up for my students. A classroom can easily become a place of violence for Black, Indigenous, and students of color through curriculum choices, the active choice of not teaching certain topics for fear of being "political," which is contradictory to the entire education system that is rooted in politics. It can be a place of fear for students who are a part of the LGBTQI+ community, especially our Black, trans students. It can be extremely challenging working at a site where a school does not provide support for their BIPOC teachers, students, and their families. Do not be afraid to ask questions about a school's commitment towards racial and social justice during your interview so you can hear directly from the hiring committee (which can include the current principal), how they are making a conscious effort to tackle these issues.

How do you determine if the culture of a building is a good fit for you?

I have worked at multiple school sites in the Inland Empire. I worked in multiple elementary schools, one middle school, and one high school. Determining whether or not the culture of a building is a good fit for me depends on the relationships I am able to build with the students/parents, staff, administration, and fellow teachers. There used to be a certain ambiance that I paid attention to, but through my education, I realized that this "ambiance" has a lot to do with a school's commitment towards being Anti-Bias/Anti-Racist. Essentially, determining whether or not a school is a good fit for you is a gut feeling. However, if you are new to a district or even state, it can be difficult to get a feel for your site. I would then recommend doing your research. Check out your site's School Accountability Report Card, LCAP, website, and social media platforms. A lot of this information is public, so you are able to view demographics and determine if this is your future workplace. I saw that my school site was mostly 80% Latinx students and I knew this would be a good place to begin my teaching career. I went in knowing that Latinx students are not a monolith, but I found comfort knowing that I was going to have students identifying as Mexican, Salvadoarian, Nicaraguan, Colombian, Honduran, Guatemalan, and so many more Latinx folks.

List three rules or pieces of advice you would give to a minority teacher entering the education field or struggling to find their way in the field.

1. Always trust your intuition and let it guide your decisions for the content you present to your students. No one knows them like you do!

2. It is perfectly OK to say "no" if something goes against your core beliefs! I know they say to nod your head and say yes to everything in your first few years of teaching, but be very clear about where you stand and set boundaries on the things that are completely non-negotiable.

3. Find a community of friends, family, or peers that will validate your feelings and experiences! If you feel a strong disconnect with certain individuals on campus or even the majority of the campus, just know there are so many communities that will support you. I turned to Instagram to find other like-minded educators as well as educators I can learn from (i.e had experience teaching with an ABAR lens) while I adjusted to my current campus. I had a space where other teachers felt the same way. It was nice to connect in a low-risk space where you know a teacher teaches in a different district, state, or even country.

[LD1]University of California?

[LD2]The rest of this sentence is missing.

REFLECTION

Brianna Moreno

WHAT PART
OF HER
OPEN LETTER
IMPACTED
YOU THE
MOST?

WHAT PIECE OF
ADVICE
DO YOU THINK
WILL HELP
YOU THE MOST
DURING YOUR
CAREER?

The following interview was conducted with Diana Maldonado.

Why did you decide to become an educator?

Most of my teachers were women; one (substitute teacher) was a black male. The first time I remember having a Latina teacher, I took to her immediately. I remember she took the time to really get to know me. I was an average student who came from an "average" home, but I still longed for some kind of attention. At that age, I was heavily into sports because that's where I felt I "belonged," where I fit. Don't get me wrong; my parents were amazing. My parents were hardworking immigrants seeking to provide for our family of six and still sent money back "home." I had what was considered a typical family: two parents, siblings, and we had just purchased our first home in the states. I was a student who loved to learn. I was, by no means, the highest performing in the class, but I certainly was *not* the lowest. I tried my best to do well and do right. I tried to make good choices. Although I was at neither end of the spectrum, my teacher took the time to get to know each and every one of her students. I was in sixth grade, and we developed a relationship I continued well into adulthood. I realized there were students who were being overlooked for one reason or another. From that, I developed a passion to support people, all kinds of people, in every facet of their lives in any way I could.

Was it your mission to serve a specific demographic (children in poverty, rural/urban environments, ELLs, special education, etc.)?

Growing up, I always thought being an "educator" meant I would be a classroom teacher. I explored other options in other industries during college, of course, but eventually took a position working with Out of School Time programs. Over the span of the next eleven years, I was an after-school instructor, a summer enrichment program counselor, an advisor, recruiter, and financial aid coordinator for an extremely competitive enrichment program that prepared students to attend a boarding school for high school and supported them to and through college. I transitioned from there to student and staff recruitment for different charter school networks. I ultimately decided I was getting farther and farther from the students, and I did not enjoy that. I finally decided to jump into the classroom after nearly twelve years of working in education. The only thing that had not changed was my desire to stay in the city in which I started my career.

Growing up in a very much working-class neighborhood, I wanted to be sure I was able to serve students who were just like me, brown students who were struggling to find their place between here and "home" or who were just looking for a place to be, students coming from families that, for one reason or another, did not know about the possibilities and opportunities that existed for their child. Let's face it: That, in and of itself, is a privilege.

Hopefully, my students' parents see I am here to simply support their efforts to educate their child. I want my students' parents to know we are in this together. I am working to support them, and this is a partnership. It is important for them to know that our lines of communication are always open. As a Spanish-speaking Latina, I can communicate a lot more with some of my students' parents, even though my Spanish is imperfect and I understand only pieces of their Portuguese.

What has been the most rewarding part of your experience as a minority teacher?

The most rewarding part of my experience is working to establish the foundation of my students' love for learning. I am currently teaching kindergarten, and for many of them, this is the first year they are in school, and we're laying a very important foundation for them. I love being able to break down some things in Spanish for my ELL learners (although I am not a "bilingual teacher").

What has been the most challenging part of your experience as a minority in education?

The challenge of spending too much out of my pocket on school supplies is a challenge all teachers face. I think, at this point, my most rewarding piece is still the most challenging part because it is *the* foundation for their experience. All students are working through challenges, but with so many coming from homes that lack resources, it puts them at a significant disadvantage. All my students have challenges they will work to overcome (parents working multiple jobs, one-parent households, illiterate parents, etc.). I am pretty certain one of them does not own a coat. Some parents may not have the time to practice letters, sight words, numbers, etc. I struggle with understanding their plight and pushing some of my students more to challenge them. I also struggle with following my heart and knowingly staying in a district that is not paying me what I need and deserve because I want to serve in a city versus a PWI.

How do you determine if the culture of a building is a good fit for you?

I am teaching kindergarten, and I love it (some days more than others). I am greeted with mostly smiles from my five-year-olds, and they challenge me in all kinds of ways. It has been far from easy, but it is great.

List three rules or pieces of advice you would give to a minority teacher entering the education field or struggling to find their way in the field.

1. Never be afraid to advocate for yourself. As a woman of color, I have always been afraid to ask for help. Everyone else asks for help; so can you. You cannot teach your students to ask for help if you do not do it first. Seek out ways to get professional development. Get to know the teachers in your school and pick their brains. Get ideas from anywhere and everywhere (social media, books, the internet). Do not be afraid to talk to your principal; mine is fantastic.

2. Work smarter, not harder. Work with your grade level. Share ideas. Plan together. I know it's hard, but it can be done. There is absolutely no reason why everyone should be spending hours and hours planning when you are all doing basically the same thing. You are stronger together.

3. I think we have been conditioned, as women and women of color in particular, to think we are not good enough. You have had a bad day, and it was the worst. You need to remember that one bad day is just one bad day. Again, teaching is tough. You'll laugh, cry, be frustrated and angry—possibly all in one day. It's OK. Really. You are enough, and you are doing a great job. Do what you need to do to stay healthy both physically and mentally. Remind yourself you are great.

Diana Maldonado

WHICH PART
OF HER STORY IMPACTED
YOU THE MOST?

WHICH PIECE OF
ADVICE DO YOU THINK
WILL HELP YOU THE MOST
DURING YOUR CAREER?

The following interview was conducted with De'Anna Baldwin.

Why did you decide to become an educator?

I became a special educator because I wanted to encourage children and help them realize they all have the ability to learn. When I was in school, the teachers who had the most impact resembled me. I wanted to be a positive representative/influencer in my community. I wanted to be a part of changing the statistical narrative that we were more likely to live in poverty. I wanted to help children realize they can be more than the labels that were placed on them.

When you decided to become a teacher, were you aware of the statistics of minority vs. non-minority teachers?

I knew when I was in graduate school that I was the only black woman in the courses. There was sometimes one other black woman in the class, and it started to alarm me. I wondered where all of the black men and women in the education field who taught me were. There had to be more. Unfortunately, there were not many more of us in the program. I researched the demographics of teachers in my school district, and we were definitely the minority.

Was it your mission to serve a specific demographic (children in poverty, rural/urban environments, ELLs, special education, etc.)?

Yes. It is my mission to serve all children, especially children with disabilities in urban areas. I believe in educating the whole child by applying theories and principles, such as meeting physical needs (food, shelter, clothing), social-emotional needs, and mental health needs. I meet all children where they are, and I do not like to focus on the end goal. I have realized that when children are enjoying themselves, they are more likely to do it again. I like to make the lessons enjoyable, so I focus them on the children's interests.

What has been the most rewarding part of your experience as a minority teacher?

The most rewarding part of my experience as a minority teacher is bonding with students and observing their progress. The students that are deemed "challenging" have the most progress at the end of the year when we, as teachers, take the time to get to know them as individuals and not by their academic progress.

What has been the most challenging part of your experience as a minority in education?

The most challenging part of my experience as a minority educator is accepting that we cannot respond in the same way as other ethnicities. When we are assertive, it is deemed "bullying, aggressive, or hard to work with," but when other ethnicities exhibit the same behaviors, it is seen as assertive. It has been one of the toughest challenges that I have yet to yield to.

How do you determine if the culture of a building is a good fit for you?

When determining if the culture of a building is a good fit for me, I look at three components: 1) Am I able to be myself? 2) Do I have room to grow here? and 3) Am I having enjoyable experiences?

Sometimes we have to consider how often we feel these experiences as well. Am I able to be myself most of the time? Am I having enjoyable experiences less than I'd like? Am I content with the growth, or lack thereof, in this placement?

List three rules or pieces of advice you would give to a minority teacher entering the education field or struggling to find their way in the field.

1. It's OK to fail. No one is perfect. Revisit why you chose to be in this field. Mistakes can be corrected.
2. Find a school that will appreciate what you have to offer.
3. Develop a self-care routine and enjoy life.

REFLECTION

De'anna Baldwin

WHAT PART **OF HER** OPEN LETTER **IMPACTED** YOU THE **MOST?**

WHAT PIECE OF **ADVICE** DO YOU THINK **WILL HELP** YOU THE MOST DURING YOUR **CAREER?**

The following interview was conducted with Nikki A., a K–12 ESE staffing specialist with twelve years of teaching experience.

Why did you decide to become an educator?

My decision to become an educator was finalized after I worked in the Child Welfare and Juvenile Justice Systems for a few years and saw that many of the concerns the children on my caseloads had were directly connected to education, or their education was heavily impacted by their circumstances and experiences (i.e., becoming wards of the state, engaging in criminal activity, joining gangs, being removed from their parents/guardians due to abuse and neglect reports, etc.).

Initially, I was told pursuing a master's degree in special education and working in the field of special education would increase my initial pay grade, so that was another deciding factor to enter the field. Unfortunately, that is not the case in the state of Florida; I was hoodwinked, bamboozled… I've come to learn that Florida doesn't compensate well for advanced degrees; it doesn't compensate teachers well at all, actually.

At first, I was afraid to go into the field of education because I was unsure of *how* to help children read. There was such a huge push in reading initiatives because children were struggling and unable to pass the FCAT (state test), and in my heart, I was sorely afraid and didn't want to "mess anyone's child up" (my exact words for years as I convinced myself to bypass education in undergrad). For me, reading was learned almost naturally as a child because I'd come from a home where education was paramount, and academics were promoted heavily by both of my parents, especially my mom. She made literacy development such a fun thing in our home, so much so that when I became of school age, learning was a joy and pleasure. I was an overachiever in every sense of the word. (I initiated a parent-teacher conference in first grade after getting a lower than expected grade on my report card. Both of my parents were expected to come so they could handle my teacher for messing my grade up. They both showed up, but the grade stayed the same.)

The children I would eventually come to teach didn't have that same experience when it came to early exposure to literacy and reading development, and that scared me tremendously because I knew how much early exposure to literacy lessened the chances of a child having a learning disability or language impairment. But by divine providence (i.e., the calling of God), I found myself interviewing for a spot in a newly formed cohort of about twenty students total at my alma mater (*The* University of South Florida, Go Bulls!) for the master's of arts in teaching varying exceptionalities, designed especially for second-career teachers looking to go into the field of special education.

Through this program, I became ESOL-endorsed and received my hours for reading endorsement. I was fully certified by the end of my program; it was a one-stop shop for everything I needed to be competitive and highly qualified in the state of Florida.

Lastly, I'd always worked with children/young people in some capacity, starting formally at age fourteen (at daycares as a teacher assistant, as an adjunct assistant, a babysitter, and as part of my church's youth group). I loved working with children because I did it well and got results, especially behaviorally. Again, I believe entering the field of education was my calling.

When you decided to become a teacher, were you aware of the statistics of minority vs. non-minority teachers?

I wasn't aware of actual numbers related to minority teachers, but by observation, it was not hard to make an informed inference on the plight of minority teachers—and minority students for that matter. I observed that, more often than not, most beginning minority teachers were placed in inner city schools. There seemed to be a very faulty perception that black and brown teachers were the only ones who could handle black and brown students behaviorally. Also, I saw minority children most commonly being identified with behavioral problems because they didn't learn traditionally like non-minority students. And on top of that, there didn't seem to be a push to try to rectify the problems; they were just overly placed into exceptional student education (ESE) programs (i.e., emotionally/behaviorally disabled, specific learning disabled, and intellectually disabled).

Was it your mission to serve a specific demographic (children in poverty, rural/urban environments, ELLs, special education, etc.)?

Yes, my mission became providing instructional excellence for children identified with disabilities because I believed *every* child I was blessed to work with could learn and grow. What a huge undertaking that was! I believe all teachers who are truly called to the profession start and work every day with that same sentiment, to give their students exactly what they need, no matter what. I don't think you ever really reach a point instructionally or in your practices and professionalism that you know you have everything every child you serve needs. There is always something more to learn for that one child, so you never stop learning, trying, attempting, researching, growing, and making yourself better in some way.

To follow through on my mission, I attended almost every training I could attend for the first five to six years of my career; I learned the importance of working alongside seasoned teachers and gleaning from their wisdom and experience, as well as sharing the newer practices I'd learned in school while training to become a "new-to-the-field" teacher. Most importantly, I dug into my students; I learned them academically, personally, mentally, and emotionally, and I learned how to meet them where they were and instruct them accordingly to get them to where they needed to be. Together, we learned to focus on closing gaps, one milestone at a time, and strived for daily small victories in the areas of deficit until we saw the changes we wanted to see.

What has been the most rewarding part of your experience as a minority teacher?

The most rewarding part of teaching has been seeing my babies do what they'd been told they would never do, seeing them overcome! I'm in my twelfth year of education, and time after time, I've watched good instruction, tough love, high and attainable expectations, collaboration between home and school, and more tough love with high expectations win their little hearts over and cause them to buy into their own education. I've watched how setting small goals, like learning ten sight words or being able to add doubles with fluency, sparks interest in the learning process and causes them to continue setting goals that lead them to overall educational success. I've had so many parents come back and say how it was those small goals and little things I did to encourage their child in their education that made a huge impact. Especially with children who have disabilities, I've learned that it's the little things that make the most difference.

What has been the most challenging part of your experience as a minority in education?

Being a minority teacher has been the greatest challenge. In terms of pedagogy, instruction, and curriculum, there seems to be the notion that white teachers are the experts, so when you're a minority educator who has an in-depth understanding of curriculum and how to effectively communicate it to students of various ability levels *and* you produce the results to back up your instructional practices, you're not taken seriously or you're bypassed and kept out of the loop. When you refuse to be denied or overlooked, your thoughts and ideas are copied, stolen, and credited to someone else, usually a white teacher you work with who can't do what you do or do it half as well as you do it.

I'd like to sidebar and say that I've worked with many white teachers. There's one lady I dubbed my "work mama" because she and I meshed so well together and developed a wonderful system that saw our students rock out and grow exponentially, general education and ESE students alike. So, obviously, not *all* white teachers can be credited with foolishness. I get that. I'm just highlighting the fact that there seems to be a pervasive practice of minimizing the effectiveness and legitimacy of minority educators in the education of all students. Side bar ended.

After so many years, you earn your "place" at the table where you've proven you are an expert in your field. Being an ESE teacher, I had to work with teachers jointly. I've had general education teachers try to make me their paraprofessional or teacher's aide, telling me they only wanted me to do this task or that (which usually ended up being something a classroom volunteer could do or behavior-related because that's what the black teacher is good at).

Many days early on in my career, I found myself addressing this situation openly and curtly: "Ma'am/Sir, I have more paper on my walls that speak to my qualifications and ability than probably anyone in this room. Don't try it." Usually, that wasn't a conversation I had to have more than once with the same person, but as I've grown as an educator and have become more settled in my instructional abilities, I've learned to just pet the data speak because, in this field, numbers speak louder and say more than I ever could.

Unfortunately, I've seen that sometimes when teachers have behaved this way, it translated into parents behaving similarly. While I might not have given the same disclaimer to parents that I gave to my colleagues, I found that letting them know how well I knew their child educationally and personally was always an eye-opener to the level of teacher and expertise they were dealing with. When you tell someone something they don't know about their child or something they knew but didn't pay attention to, it has a way of making them listen. Because I love my babies, I've often found I was the teacher being talked about when the kids went home, and parents were often wondering who it was that was having such an influence on their child. Lo and behold, the black lady you thought was just a paraprofessional is the one impacting your child's whole life. Figure that.

How do you determine if the culture of a building is a good fit for you?

I've only worked in four schools in my twelve years. I'm not one that runs from adversity. As far as school culture and climate, I believe everyone has a part to play in it. As long as you're actively doing your part to enhance the culture, it should be the culture for you. Don't complain about problems you haven't actively worked to find solutions for. Just don't. My last placement was absolutely horrible, but I worked daily and did my part to help make my class, team, and school the best it could be, despite opposition. When I knew I'd done all I could, I believe God honored that and moved me. It took a while for me to learn how to contribute and be a part of the solutions, despite being taken for granted and working alongside people who didn't always have the same work ethic as me. But I had to learn to work through it and do what needed to be done for my students, no matter what. Sometimes people don't want to change or grow, but don't allow that to stop you. Bloom wherever you're planted. Be the rose that grew from the concrete.

List three rules or pieces of advice you would give to a minority teacher entering the education field or struggling to find their way in the field.

1. Never judge your effectiveness as a teacher until after the year has ended. Children grow at differing rates according to their ability, the level of outside support, and a billion other factors that impact their education. If you measure yourself in the middle of the year while your children are required to make a year's worth of growth, you're shortchanging yourself. Give yourself space and time to grow with them, and after you say your final "goodbye," then you can self-evaluate what you did great, what you did well, what you did alright, and what you need to trash before the next year.

2. Be willing to grow! Education is not a field you can pull up and park in one thought, practice, strategy, belief, or mindset because this field and the expectations of educators change daily. Our

children come with different issues every day that require us to be on our toes and be flexible to adequately address the needs they have that day and in that moment. If we're unyielding and inflexible in our practices, we will easily miss the opportunities presented to us to help make their lives better.

3. While you're growing, don't forget to be anchored. Yes, you have to grow; however, some practices should be mainstays in your daily routine and how you engage with your children. Be anchored in the things that make your babies better human beings who will contribute to this world in a positive way. Be anchored in love, no matter the child, no matter the difficulty they present, no matter the problems and challenges they experience or cause. Let them always know that your love for them is constant. Be anchored in professionalism and display yourself as the best educator you can be in front of your students, their families, the community, and your colleagues. Be anchored.

REFLECTION

Nikki A.

WHICH PART
OF HER STORY IMPACTED
YOU THE MOST?

WHICH PIECE OF
ADVICE DO YOU THINK
WILL HELP YOU THE MOST
DURING YOUR CAREER?

This interview was conducted with Analise Harris, a middle/high school special education teacher and adjunct professor, with eight years of experience and an MA in Education.

Why did you decide to become an educator?

I learned through my formative years in education that there were significant differences within classrooms, let alone different schools. Being a black student identified as gifted and talented, I recognized that my classes were full of white students, and my friends were in other classes across the hall. This early introduction to the tracking system is what led me to realize that the ways I was allowed to learn, fail, express myself, and thrive in my special tracked classes were not the same for my peers, and I believe all students deserve to have the freedom I experienced. That memory held me to a very high standard where I recognized my gift of working with students who were on IEPs in special education.

After graduating from college, I realized that despite having a degree and many achievements on paper, without a career, I had little purpose. Looking for a job as a recent college graduate during a recession was very disappointing. After soul-searching, I considered what type of lifestyle I really wanted for myself, which included whether I wanted kids, if I wanted to live near family, and what I was even relatively good at that could make a sustainable life. I also considered that I wanted to be able to enjoy my summers, I was good with kids during summer camps, and I enjoyed planning events and performing. I thought about what I did not enjoy, which was food service and folding clothes, as well as being told what to do every day. With those factors swirling around, I realized I could probably be good at teaching, and summertime freedom sounded like an untapped field. At that moment, I did not have a clue how much a teacher made in relation to how much the cost of living was truly going to be wherever I taught. I looked into how to become a teacher, saw an opportunity to become a substitute teacher at the same schools I walked the halls of, and thought making one hundred dollars a day could really pan out, and I would also get to choose my assignments and have a great schedule of my choice. Little did I know how much I would be learning, creating, and applying my social justice work and passions into my career.

When you decided to become a teacher, were you aware of the statistics of minority vs. non-minority teachers?

I don't believe it truly resonated how severely lacking the minority teacher vs. other teachers ratio was until I began my second year of teaching. Living in a state that has a very low black population in general, I suppose I was just accustomed to the whiteness. It was not until I faced opposition regarding ways to recognize Black History Month that I realized I was not in "Oz's Kansas" anymore. Internal questions arose regarding who was not handling their classroom management, why I had to be the one to talk with certain students, how to uphold IEP goals with new staff, and which teachers were not nice to students.

Was it your mission to serve a specific demographic (children in poverty, rural/urban environments, ELLs, special education, etc.)?

I consider special education to be a spectrum, so my decision to become a special education teacher was a way to pay homage to the individuals who taught me and share the love of learning I had with a vulnerable population who typically would not say they felt the same way about school.

What has been the most rewarding part of your experience as a minority teacher?

In the past year, I've actually run into former students while I have been out in the community and received phone calls from parents thanking me for inspiring them or just holding them to a high standard.

What has been the most challenging part of your experience as a minority in education?

As a black special education teacher, recruiter, and adjunct professor for concurrent enrollment, as well as community college courses, one of the most difficult aspects of this experience in education is deciding when to push an issue and when to play by the rules. Another challenge that weighs heavily is concerning my consciousness in upholding certain rules I do not believe truly put the needs of students first.

How do you determine if the culture of a building is a good fit for you?

I vet a building environment by assessing how deeply the administrators rely on data, which data they assess, and what investments are made to make the space welcoming to all visitors. Additionally, I inquire about their meeting schedules. Too many meetings is a red flag for me, and not enough relevant core team meetings is a sign of poor structure. As an educator and creative person, I appreciate buildings where teachers have opportunities to include their own hobbies into the building. An easy example would be a teacher who paints outside of school hours being able to support students in painting a mural for the building.

List three rules or pieces of advice you would give to a minority teacher entering the education field or struggling to find their way within the field.

1. Stay true to your authentic self.

2. Remember you are providing the education you would have wanted to receive as a young learner.

3. Nobody remembers how bomb that lesson was; they'll remember the support you gave them and the chance they had to love learning.

REFLECTION

Analise Harris

WHAT PART
OF HER
INTERVIEW
IMPACTED
YOU THE
MOST?

WHAT PIECE OF
ADVICE
DO YOU THINK
WILL HELP
YOU THE MOST
DURING YOUR
CAREER?

Potential Interview Questions

1. How do you train your staff to construct culturally responsive classrooms?

2. Does the district offer opportunities for diversity training?

3. What is the teacher retention rate?

4. What are students most in need of at the moment?

5. What resources are available for new teachers?

6. Will I be given a mentor? How often will we meet?

7. Are there trainings available to new teachers?

8. If possible, tour the school and meet the staff. Ask to observe the classroom of an exemplary teacher.

Thank you to each and every educator who shared their stories. I am tremendously grateful for your vulnerability and advice.

Printed in Great Britain
by Amazon

41350643R00053